People of the Bible

The Bible through stories and pictures

Samson and Delilah

Copyright © in this format Belitha Press Ltd, 1986

Text copyright © Catherine Storr 1986

Illustrations copyright © Ivan Lapper 1986

Art Director: Treld Bicknell

First published in the United States of America 1986
by Raintree Publishers Inc.
310 West Wisconsin Avenue, Milwaukee, Wisconsin 53203
in association with Belitha Press Ltd, London.

Conceived, designed and produced by Belitha Press Ltd,
2 Beresford Terrace, London N5 2DH

ISBN 0-8172-2044-5 (U.S.A.)

Library of Congress Cataloging in Publication Data

Storr, Catherine.
  Samson and Delilah.

  (People of the Bible)
  Summary: Recounts the Old Testament story of
Samson's remarkable strength and Delilah's betrayal
of him to the Philistines.
    1. Samson (Biblical judge)—Juvenile literature.
2. Delilah (Biblical figure) Juvenile literature.
[1. Samson (Biblical judge) 2. Delilah (Biblical
figure) 3. Bible stories—O.T.] I. Title.
II. Series.
BS580.S15S69   1985   222'.3209505   85-12287

ISBN 0-8172-2044-5

First published in Great Britain in hardback 1986
by Franklin Watts Ltd,
12a Golden Square, London W1R 4BA

 4 5 6 7 8 9 10 11 12 13   98 99 97 96 95 94 93 92 91 90 89

Samson and Delilah

Retold by Catherine Storr
Pictures by Ivan Lapper

Raintree Childrens Books
Milwaukee
Belitha Press Limited • London

For forty years, the children of Israel were ruled by the Philistines, their enemies. During this time, an angel of God appeared to Manoah, an Israelite man, and told him that he was going to have a son. This son would deliver the Israelites from the Philistines. He was to be brought up as a Nazarite, set apart to serve God. As a sign that his life belonged to God, he should never have his hair cut nor his beard shaved. Manoah's son was born and was called Samson.

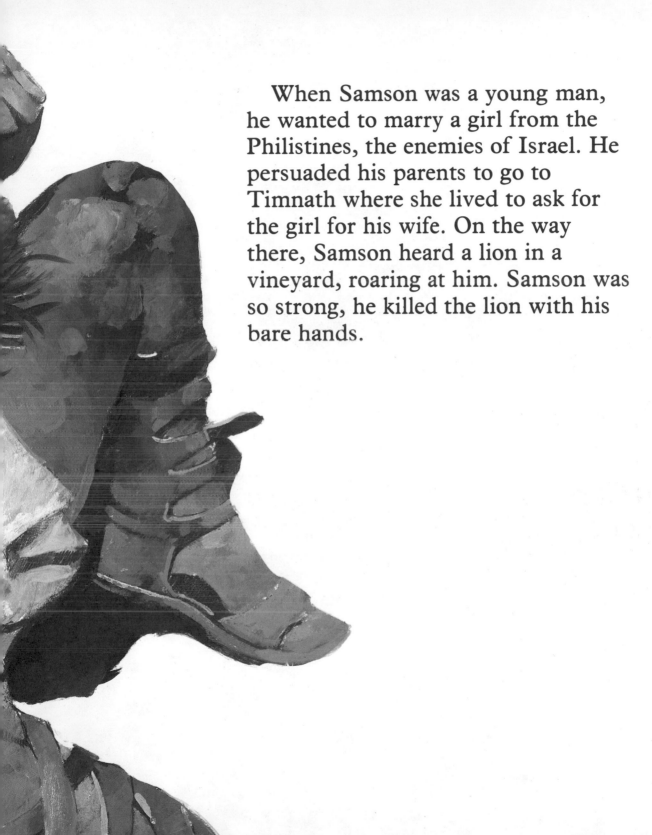

When Samson was a young man, he wanted to marry a girl from the Philistines, the enemies of Israel. He persuaded his parents to go to Timnath where she lived to ask for the girl for his wife. On the way there, Samson heard a lion in a vineyard, roaring at him. Samson was so strong, he killed the lion with his bare hands.

8

The wedding was arranged. When Samson was returning to Timnath for the feast, he went to see what had happened to the dead lion. A swarm of bees had settled in the lion's body. Samson took some of the honey they had made.

The wedding feast lasted for seven days.
Samson told a riddle to the young Philistine
men there.

He said, "If you can answer this riddle, I
will give you presents. But if you can't, you
will have to pay me." This was the riddle:
Out of the eater there came meat, and out
of the strong there came forth sweetness.

None of the young men
could answer the riddle. They
said secretly to Samson's bride,
"You must find out the
answer, and tell us. If you
don't, we will burn you and
your father's house."

The bride said to Samson, "You don't love me, or you would have told me about this riddle which you have asked of my people."

Samson said, "I haven't even told my father and mother."

But his bride would not let him rest. She went on begging for the answer. At last Samson told her, and she told the young men.

The young men said to Samson, "We can answer your riddle. What is sweeter than honey? What is stronger than a lion?"

Samson was very angry. He said, "My bride has told you the answer."

Then he left his bride in Timnath and went back to his own father's house.

16

After a time, Samson went back to Timnath for his bride. But her father said, "You went away and left her. Now I have given her as a wife to someone else."

This made Samson so angry that he set fire to the Philistines' fields and to their vines and olive trees. The Philistines came to Judea for their revenge.

The Israelites said to Samson, "Why did you set fire to their fields, when you know that they rule over us?"

Samson said, "All I did was to pay them back for what they had done to me. Don't kill me."

The Israelites did not kill him, but they bound him and handed him over to the Philistines. Samson was so strong that without difficulty he broke the ropes that bound him, as if they were only burned threads. Then he picked up the jawbone of an ass and killed a great number of his enemies.

After this, Samson fell in love with another woman who was also a Philistine, called Delilah. The Philistine lords said to Delilah, "When you are married to Samson, find out the secret of his great strength, so that we may overcome him. If you do this, each one of us will give you eleven hundred pieces of silver."

Delilah asked Samson, "Please tell me what makes you so strong."

Samson said, "If I were bound with seven green reeds, I should lose all my strength."

When he was asleep, Delilah bound Samson with seven fresh green reeds. She called out, "The Philistines are upon you, Samson!" Samson woke, and broke the reeds as if they had been threads.

Delilah asked Samson again, "What makes you so strong?"

Samson said, "I shouldn't be strong if I were bound with new ropes that had never been used."

When Samson was asleep, Delilah again bound him with new ropes. But Samson broke these too.

The third time, Delilah
bound Samson's hair in a
web and tied the web to a
beam of wood. But when he
woke, Samson broke the
web and the beam.

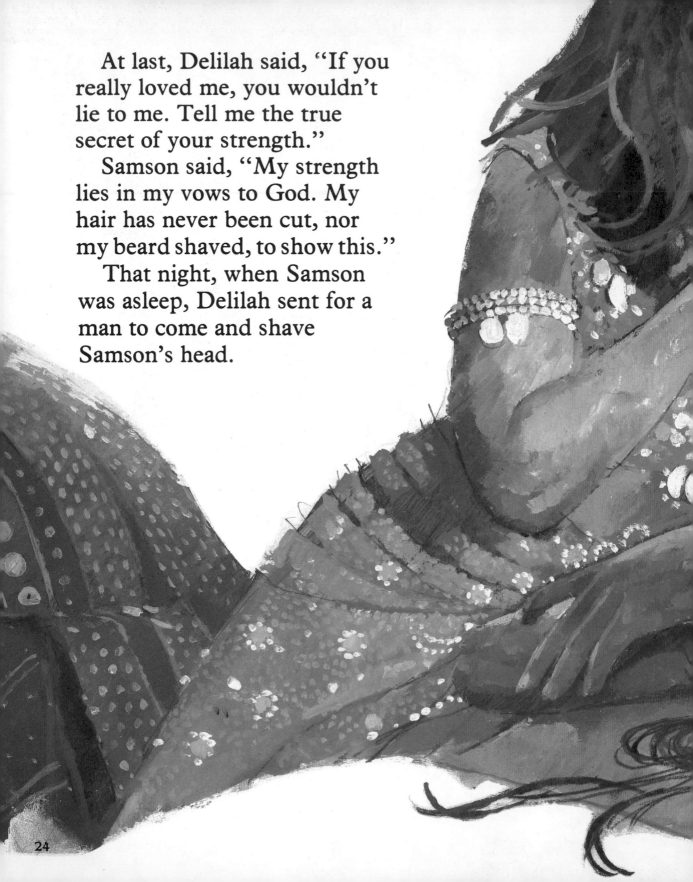

At last, Delilah said, "If you really loved me, you wouldn't lie to me. Tell me the true secret of your strength."

Samson said, "My strength lies in my vows to God. My hair has never been cut, nor my beard shaved, to show this."

That night, when Samson was asleep, Delilah sent for a man to come and shave Samson's head.

When Samson woke, he found that his
strength had left him. The Philistine lords
took him prisoner. They took him to Gaza
where they put out his eyes. They bound
him with chains of brass and threw him
into prison. But his hair began to grow
again.

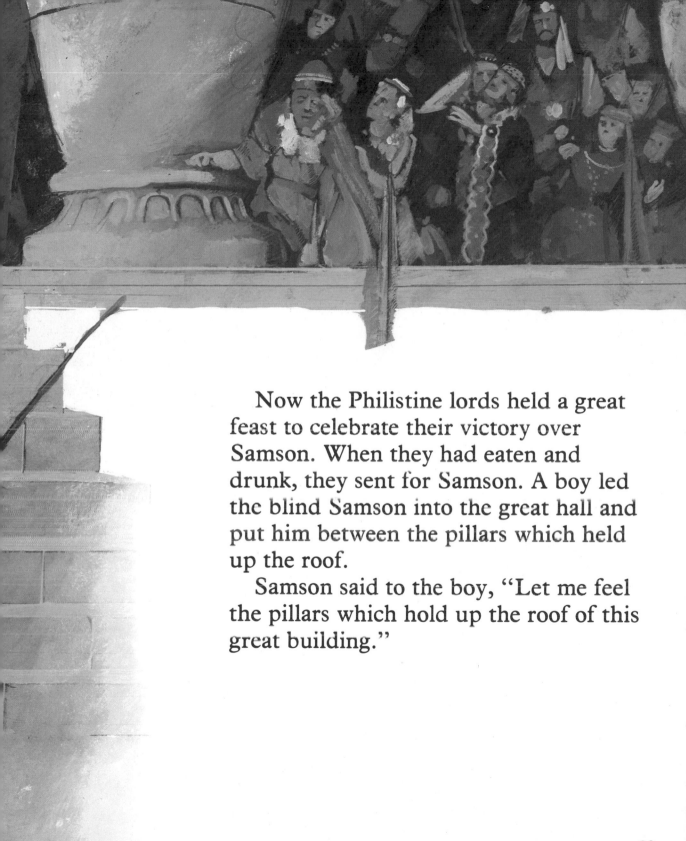

Now the Philistine lords held a great feast to celebrate their victory over Samson. When they had eaten and drunk, they sent for Samson. A boy led the blind Samson into the great hall and put him between the pillars which held up the roof.

Samson said to the boy, "Let me feel the pillars which hold up the roof of this great building."

When his hands were on the pillars, Samson prayed to God, "Give me back my strength, Lord, so that I may be revenged on my enemies."

God heard his prayer and gave him strength. Samson put his hands on the pillars and bowed himself down and pushed with all his might. The pillars broke, and the roof fell in and killed him and all the people there. So, in his death, Samson conquered the Philistines.

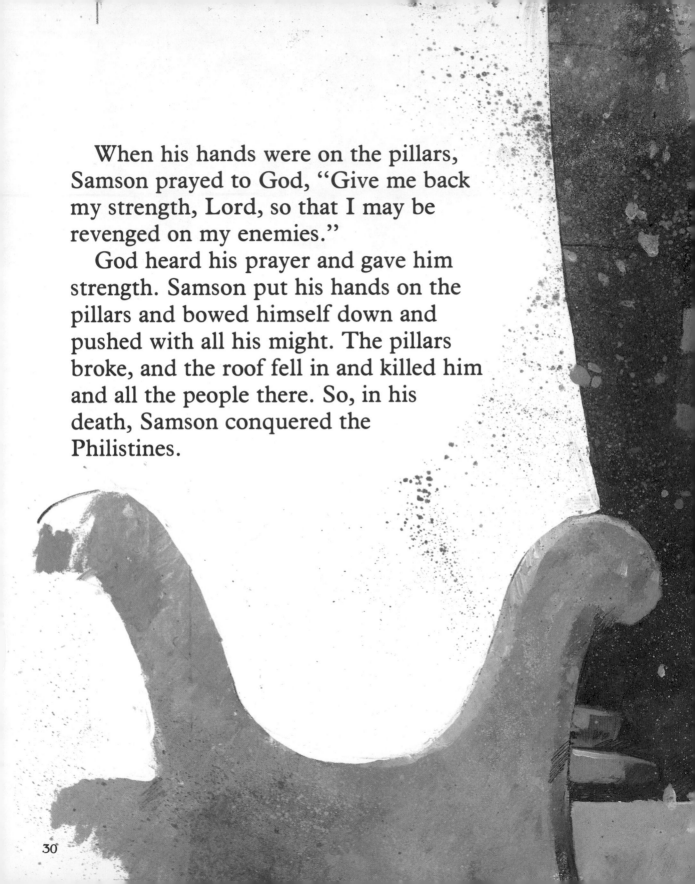

31

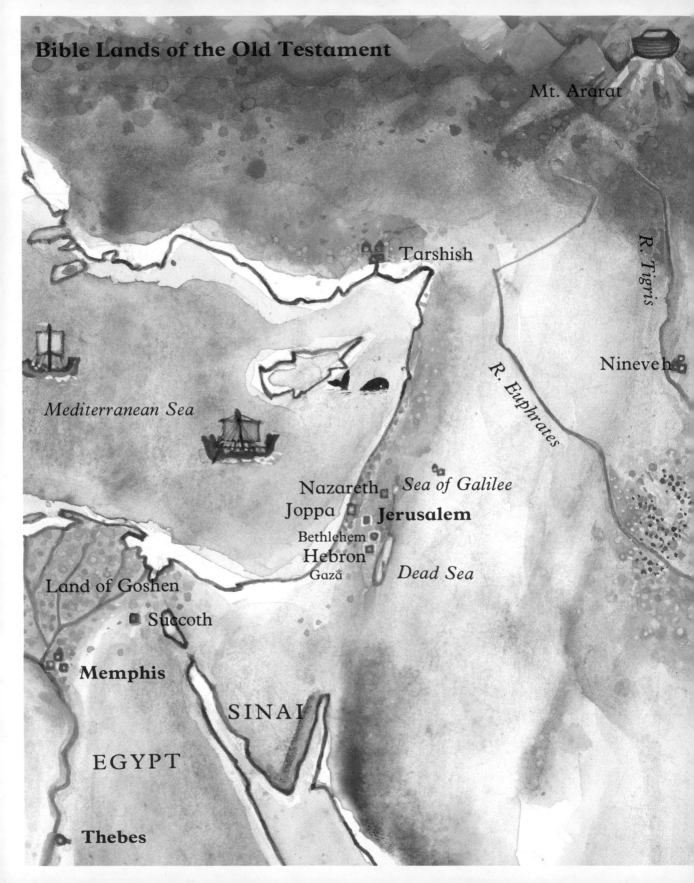

Bible Lands of the Old Testament

Mt. Ararat

R. Tigris

Tarshish

Nineveh

R. Euphrates

Mediterranean Sea

Nazareth

Sea of Galilee

Joppa

Jerusalem

Bethlehem

Hebron

Gaza

Dead Sea

Land of Goshen

Succoth

Memphis

SINAI

EGYPT

Thebes